THE STAR WARS® COOKBOOK II

DARTH MALT AND MORE RECIPES

BY FRANKIE FRANKENY
AND WESLEY MARTIN

PHOTOGRAPHY BY
FRANKIE FRANKENY

chronicle books · san francisco

All figures and vehicles courtesy of Hasbro, Inc.
Jell-O® is a registered trademark of Kraft Foods, Inc.

Art direction and concepts by Frankie Frankeny and Wesley Martin.
Food styling by Wesley Martin.
Props by Camella Haecker.
Series design by Daniel Carter.
Book design by Paul Donald|Graphic Detail.
Typeset in Bell Gothic, Clicker and Univers.

The photographer wishes to thank my partner in this project Wesley Martin, Jennifer
Vetter and Mikyla Bruder at Chronicle Books for their help on a challenging project,
Larry and Angela Tse, JoAnn Frankeny, Larry Van and Pete Zimmerhanzel of Taylor
Meat for their awesome foot-long hotdogs, Anne Schlatter at Pro Camera for her
Podracer mechanics, and especially Leslie Jonath and Erica Jacobs who started all
this fun photography with their belief in *Wookiee Cookies*.

Chronicle Books and the authors would also like to thank Jane Mason, Sarah Hines
Stephens, Ben Harper, and Iain Morris at Lucasfilm, Linda Bickel at Hasbro, and
Olivia Evans.

Library of Congress Cataloging-in-Publication Data available.
ISBN-10 0-8118-2803-4
ISBN-13 978-0-8118-2803-1

Printed in Malaysia.
10 9 8 7 6 5 4

Chronicle Books
680 Second Street, San Francisco, California 94107

www.chroniclekids.com
www.starwars.com

Table of Contents

Introduction

Always two there are...

The *Star Wars Cookbook: Wookiee Cookies and Other Galactic Recipes* guided you on a culinary journey through the swamps of Dagobah and the icy realms of Hoth. Now, young Padawan, it is clear that you are the chosen one—the one who will bring balance to the kitchen—and it is time to prepare yourself for a new challenge ... *The Star Wars Cookbook II: Darth Malt and More Galactic Recipes*, a book full of culinary adventures from the lush forests of Naboo, the sand-scoured outskirts of Tattooine, and the bustling city planet of Coruscant.

Some of the recipes here are simple enough to make on your own for yourself and for friends, while others require the help of a Master of the Force (sometimes known as Mom or Dad). In any case, it's always best to consult with an adult before trying something new. Adults, like Jedi Masters, know a great deal about the mysteries of the Force, and will be able to guide you in your culinary pursuits.

Whatever adventures you choose, remember that cooking should always be fun, always be safe, and that the wisdom of the second *Star Wars* Cookbook is meant to help you find your way.

BEFORE YOU BEGIN

It is important that you master some basic safety steps before you begin any project in the kitchen.
1. An adult should always be present when you're cooking, especially if you are using knives, the stovetop, the oven, or tricky gadgets like food processors or blenders. Think of yourself as a Jedi apprentice, and of the adult as the Jedi Master. There's a lot of good stuff to learn from a Master.
2. Shmi Skywalker would tell you to wash your hands well with soap and warm water before handling food or kitchen tools.

While you're cooking, stay alert. Reach out with your senses, and you'll find that you are able to prevent most kitchen mishaps. Here are some golden rules:

CONCENTRATE ON THE MOMENT

▶ Never run in the kitchen.

▶ Always wear shoes in the kitchen.

▶ Always keep everything—potholders, towels, packages of ingredients, this book, your fingers—away from burners on the stove. And remember, the stove may be hot even if the burners aren't on.

▶ Dry your hands thoroughly before turning on any electric switch or putting in or pulling out a plug.

▶ Wash knives and other sharp utensils one at a time. Don't drop them in a pan or bucket of soapy water—you may cut yourself when you reach into the water.

▶ Lift the lids of hot pots at an angle away from you, directing the rising steam away from your face.

▶ Use only dry potholders. Wet ones will conduct heat quickly and may burn you when you touch the handle of a hot pot.

▶ Put a pot or pan on the stove before you turn on the heat.

▶ Turn off the heat before you remove a pot or pan from the stove.

▶ Never put out a grease fire with water. Water causes grease to splatter and can spread the fire very quickly. To put out a grease fire, smother it with a tight-fitting lid or throw handfuls of baking soda onto it.

ACT WISELY

▶ Never leave the kitchen while something is cooking.

▶ Keep pot handles away from the edge of the stove so the pots aren't easily toppled.

▶ Always position pot handles away from other stove burners. Otherwise, they'll get hot and burn you.

▶ Remove utensils from hot pots when you're not using them, placing them on a plate or spoon holder near the stove. Metal spoons and spatulas are especially dangerous because they'll absorb the heat and burn your hand when you go to use them.

▶ Start with a clean kitchen and keep it clean as you cook. If something spills, wipe it up right away. If you have time, wash dishes as you go.

▶ Turn off the blender's motor before removing the lid.

▶ Put ingredients away when you're finished with them.

▶ Know where to find the fire extinguisher and be sure it's in working order.

▶ Keep the fire department's number next to the phone.

The tools of the *Darth Malt* chef are powerful. Everything has a purpose. Treat all cooking equipment with the utmost respect, and use items only for their intended purpose. Here's a list of what you may need:

TOOLS
Aluminum foil
Baking dishes
Baking sheets
Blender*
Cake pan
Can opener
Cheese grater
Colander
Cookie cutters
Cooling rack
Cutting board
Electric mixer*
Food processor*
Ice-cream scoop
Ice-cream maker
Knives*

Ladle
Measuring cups and spoons
Mixing bowls of various sizes
Oven mitts
Paper cups
Parchment paper
(for lining baking sheets)
Pastry brush
Plastic wrap
Pizza pan
Potholders
Rolling pin
Rubber and metal spatulas
Saucepans with lids
Sauté pan
Stockpot
Strainer
Sifter
Skewers*
Skillet
Tongs
Toothpicks
Vegetable peeler
Vegetable steamer
Waffle iron
Whisk
Wooden spoons
Zip-lock bags

*Use these items with extreme caution, and only with the help of a Master of the Force (Mom or Dad).

Go forth, young Jedi! May your Panakacakes be peanutty, may your Watto-melon Cubes be lucky, and may the Force always be with you!

Breakfasts

7

Sith Speeder Sunrise

If you want to know the secret behind Darth Maul's dexterity and determination, you just might find it in this nutritious breakfast. This wholesome speeder slice of juicy melon atop a dune of sweet, creamy oatmeal will keep you zipping around all day long.

INGREDIENTS

1½	cups milk
1	tablespoon honey
½	teaspoon cinnamon
¾	cup rolled oats
2	1-inch wedges cantaloupe

1. In a saucepan, bring the milk, honey, and cinnamon to a boil.
2. Add the oats and simmer for 6 to 8 minutes, stirring occasionally.
3. Transfer the oats to a bowl.
4. Cut a 1-inch-square piece of cantaloupe from one of the wedges and slice a V shape out of the melon without cutting through the rind.
5. Push the square "power pack" onto one end of the other melon wedge. You can secure it by driving a toothpick through the wedge and the power pack square.
6. Place the melon speeder on top of the "sand dune" of oatmeal and enjoy!
Serves 1

Boonta Classic Waffles

Start your engines with a winning plateful of these crisp golden waffles. Delicious served with Banana Butter.

WAFFLES

$1\frac{1}{2}$ cups all-purpose flour

1   tablespoon baking powder

1   tablespoon sugar

1   tablespoon brown sugar

$\frac{1}{2}$ teaspoon salt

3   large eggs

2   tablespoons melted butter

$1\frac{1}{2}$ cups milk

1   teaspoon vanilla

BANANA BUTTER

4   tablespoons butter, at room temperature

1   teaspoon sugar

1   ripe banana

$\frac{1}{2}$ cup crushed pistachios, walnuts, and pecans

$\frac{1}{4}$ teaspoon cinnamon

1. Preheat waffle iron (a Belgian iron with large squares is best).
2. In a large bowl, whisk together the dry ingredients. Make a well in the center.
3. In a separate bowl, whisk together the eggs, butter, milk, and vanilla, then pour into the well of the dry ingredients.
4. With a wooden spoon, mix the batter until just combined. (A few lumps are okay.)
5. Pour $\frac{1}{4}$ to $\frac{1}{2}$ cup batter into the hot iron and close the lid. Cook for 4 to 5 minutes, or until brown and crisp. Remove the waffle and repeat until batter is used up.
6. Spread the Banana Butter on the warm waffles.
7. Use crushed pistachios, walnuts, and pecans to make the spectators at the Podrace.

To make Banana Butter:
1. With a mixer, whip the butter, sugar and cinnamon together until soft.
2. In a separate bowl, mash the banana with a fork.
3. Add the banana to the butter mixture and whip until smooth.
Serves 6

Forceful Frittata

How feel you? Well, you'll feel *great* after a slice of this frittata. An elegant family breakfast, it's reminiscent of the decorative floor of the Jedi Council Chamber, where the great Jedi Masters convene to discuss the workings of the galaxy.

INGREDIENTS

6	eggs
1/2	cup milk
1/2	cup shredded mozzarella, 1 teaspoon reserved for topping
1/2	teaspoon salt
1/2	teaspoon pepper
1/2	cup of your favorite marinara sauce
15-20	fresh basil leaves

1. Preheat oven to 375°F.

2. Generously grease an 8-inch round cake pan.

3. In a large bowl, whisk together the eggs, milk, mozzarella (reserving 1 teaspoon), salt, and pepper.

4. Pour the egg mixture into cake pan and bake for 30 minutes on center oven rack. The edges of the frittata will just begin to brown.

5. Remove from oven and allow to cool for 2 to 3 minutes.

6. Place a flat plate or tray over the cake pan and flip the frittata onto the plate.

7. Spread the marinara sauce in the center of the frittata in a 3-inch circle. Sprinkle the reserved teaspoon of shredded mozzarella on the tomato sauce, and place the basil leaves around the edges to recreate the Jedi Chamber floor.

8. Cut into wedges and serve.

Serves 4 to 6

Booma Breakfast Tarts

Organic energy gives the Booma their mysterious power. You can energize yourself with these delicious breakfast tarts!

INGREDIENTS

1	egg
3	tablespoons sugar
1	frozen pie-crust shell, thawed
$\frac{1}{4}$	cup blueberry jam
1	tube lavender cake-decorating icing with a small tip (optional)

1. Preheat oven to 375°F.
2. Crack the egg into a small bowl and beat it with a fork until well mixed.
3. Sprinkle 1 tablespoon of the sugar on the work surface.
4. Turn the pie-crust shell over onto the sugared work surface. Carefully press the crust down, being careful not to tear it. Sprinkle another tablespoon of sugar on top of the crust. With a rolling pin, gently roll over the crust to press the sugar in—try not to roll the crust any thinner.
5. Using a large oval cookie cutter, cut out six ovals. Transfer three to a parchment-lined baking sheet. With a pastry brush, brush egg mixture around the edges of each oval, covering only about $\frac{1}{4}$ inch of the edge with egg. Place 1 teaspoon of the jam on each oval and spread it out to where the egg wash begins.
6. With the smallest round cookie cutter you have, or a small knife, cut a small circle out of three of the ovals right in the center. Place these three ovals over the first three ovals. With your finger, gently press the edges of the tart together to seal them.
7. Brush the top of each tart with the remaining egg mixture. Sprinkle additional sugar on each tart.
8. Bake for 15 minutes, or until golden brown.
9. Decorate with the icing after tarts have cooled.
Makes 3 tarts

Handmaiden Hash Browns

These savory hash browned potatoes have an understated elegance, just like the handmaidens. Wedges of this crispy potato cake make a fantastic accompaniment to a slice of Forceful Fritatta.

INGREDIENTS

2	large russet potatoes
1	small red pepper, seeded and finely chopped
2	tablespoons vegetable oil
	Salt
	Pepper
	Grated cheddar cheese (optional)

1. Peel the potatoes and rinse in cold water.

2. Grate the potatoes using the large holes on a cheese grater, or a food processor fitted with a grater attachment. Keep your fingers away from the grater! Place the grated potatoes in a colander, rinse well with cold water, and drain. Toss with the chopped red pepper.

3. Heat 1 tablespoon of the oil in a large skillet over medium heat. Spread the grated potatoes in a thin, even layer in the skillet. Using a spatula, press the potatoes into the pan. Fry the potatoes for approximately 8 minutes, or until the bottom turns golden brown.

4. Remove the pan from the heat. Place a large plate or tray over the skillet and carefully flip the potato cake onto the plate. Pour the remaining tablespoon of oil onto the skillet. Carefully slide the potato cake into the pan so the unbrowned side faces down. Return skillet to the heat. Fry for another 8 minutes, or until the other side turns golden brown.

5. Season to taste with salt and pepper. Sprinkle with cheese, if desired. Cut into wedges and serve.

Serves 4

Snacks and Sides

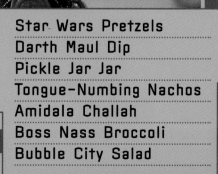

Star Wars Pretzels

Crispy on the outside and soft on the inside, these salty and delectable pretzels take on added magic when they spell out those two winning words: *Star Wars*.

INGREDIENTS

1	package (11 ounces) refrigerator bread sticks (8 sticks of dough)
1/4	cup water
2	tablespoons coarse salt crystals

1. Preheat oven to 375°F.

2. Open bread-stick package, unroll dough, and separate.

3. On a parchment-lined baking sheet, spell out S-T-A-R W-A-R-S with the dough. It should take one bread stick per letter. Cut the dough when necessary to make the letters.

4. Brush each letter with water and sprinkle coarse salt all over the letters.

5. Bake for 10 to 15 minutes, until golden brown.

6. Arrange the letters on a dark-colored plate or platter (if you have one) and serve with mustard. You can also sprinkle coarse salt on the plate to make the stars.

Darth Maul Dip

This recipe can easily be doubled or tripled for a party. Use the template at the back of this book.

INGREDIENTS

1	jar (15 ounces) roasted red peppers
1	small clove garlic, peeled
1	teaspoon red wine vinegar
1/2	teaspoon salt
1/2	teaspoon pepper
1	tablespoon cream cheese
2	pearl onions
1/4	cup poppy seeds
	Corn chips or crackers

1. With a colander or sifter, drain the peppers. Lay them flat on a piece of paper towel. Blot the peppers to dry them as much as possible. Remove any pieces of blackened skin.
2. Place the peppers and all remaining ingredients, except the pearl onions and poppy seeds, in a blender or food processor and blend until smooth.
3. Use a spatula to spread the dip evenly onto a flat plate that is larger than the Darth Maul template. Chill the dip for 1 hour.
4. Remove the chilled dip from the refrigerator and lay the template over the dip. Sprinkle the poppy seeds evenly it. Brush off any poppy seeds lying on the template and carefully lift up the template.
5. Place the pearl onions on the face to make eyes, adding one poppy seed on each onion for the pupils. (You can make Darth Maul's eyes yellow by soaking the onions in warm water with a pinch of saffron.)
6. Place three or four corn chips into the head for horns.
7. Place the dip on the table and drape a black cloth around the plate to make Darth Maul's cape.
8. Serve with corn chips or crackers.
Makes 1 1/2 cups

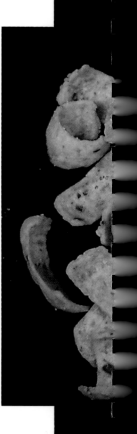

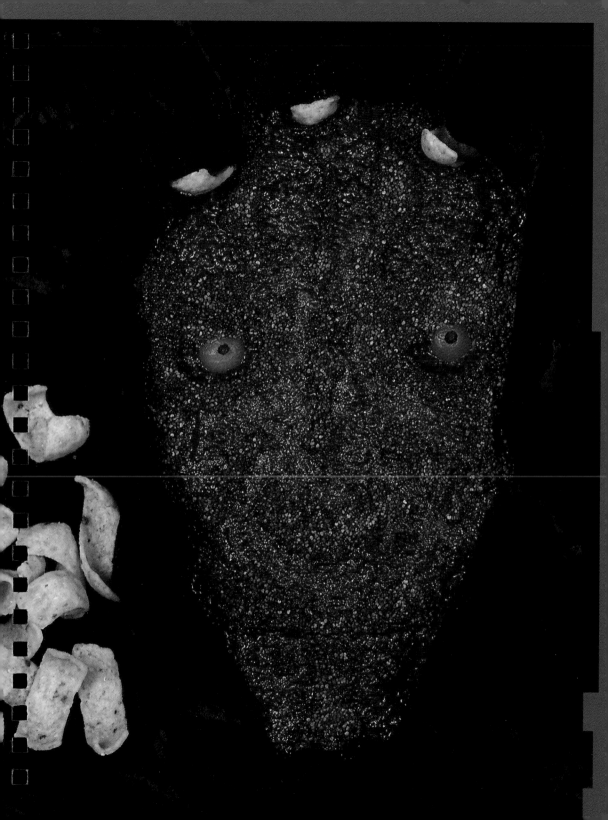

Pickle Jar Jar

Jar Jar shouldn't have any trouble getting his tongue around these sweet-and-sour refrigerator pickles, and neither should you.

INGREDIENTS

2	cups distilled white vinegar
1	cup sugar
2	large cucumbers
3	large carrots, peeled
2	cloves fresh garlic

1. In a large bowl, whisk together the vinegar and sugar until dissolved.

2. Wash the cucumbers and carrots. Cut each cucumber in half lengthwise, then each half into three spears. Cut the carrots in half lengthwise, then each half again lengthwise. Trim the carrots to fit the jar you use.

3. Pack the cucumbers and carrots together in quart-size jars. (Mayonnaise jars work great. You'll need two for this recipe.) Slice the garlic cloves into thin slices and add to each jar. Pour the liquid over the cucumbers and carrots until completely covered. If you run out of liquid, top off each jar with cool water.

4. Refrigerate for at least 2 days.

5. Remove cucumbers and carrots from jars with a fork or your fingers and enjoy!

Makes 2 quart jars

Tongue-Numbing Nachos

This wondrous pile of tortilla chips, beans, lettuce, cheese, and olives will satisfy any appetite, extraterrestrial or otherwise. But be cautious with the jalapeños. Too many of those can be as dangerous as Podracing!

INGREDIENTS

½	bag (14 ounces) tortilla chips
1	can (15 ounces) refried beans
½	cup of your favorite salsa
1	cup shredded jack or cheddar cheese, or a combination of both
1	small can sliced black olives, drained
1	tablespoon jarred jalapeños, diced
1	cup shredded lettuce

1. Preheat oven to 350°F.
2. On a large cookie sheet, arrange the chips in one even layer.
3. In a bowl, stir the refried beans with 1 tablespoon of the salsa to thin them. With a spoon, drop the beans onto the chips as evenly as possible.
4. Sprinkle the cheese evenly over the beans. Then sprinkle the olives and diced jalapeños over the top of the cheese.
5. Bake for 12 to 15 minutes, or until cheese is melted and bubbly.
6. Remove from oven. Sprinkle the lettuce and remaining salsa over the top.
7. Serve using a spatula.
Serves 4 to 6

Amidala Challah

This recipe is no cakewalk—it will take about 5 hours total. But if you have some time on your hands and a little patience, you can make two beautiful loaves of braided, buttery bread fit for a queen. Be sure to ask your Jedi Master for help!

INGREDIENTS

2	tablespoons yeast
2 1/4	cups lukewarm water
2/3	cup maple syrup
3	beaten eggs
1/2	cup butter
1	tablespoon salt
7-8	cups unbleached all-purpose flour
1	beaten egg for wash
1	tablespoon poppy seeds and/or sesame seeds
1	teaspoon coarse salt

1. Dissolve the yeast in the water. Add the maple syrup, eggs (reserving 2 tablespoons), butter, and salt and mix well.
2. Gradually add the flour.
3. Knead the dough on a floured board until elastic, about 8 minutes. Place in a greased bowl and cover with a cloth. Let the dough rise until doubled, about 1 hour.
4. Divide the dough into six parts. Roll three parts into long strips and braid together, sealing the ends to make one loaf. Repeat with the remaining three parts.
5. Cover the loaves with cloth and allow to rise until doubled.
6. Preheat oven to 350°F.
7. Brush with beaten egg wash and sprinkle with seeds and salt.
8. Bake on a greased sheet for 45 to 50 minutes, until golden brown. With oven mitts, carefully lift one loaf and tap the bottom with your knuckle. It will make a hollow thudding sound if it's done.
Makes 2 loaves

Boss Nass Broccoli

Here's a secret: when Boss Nass was a little Gungan, he didn't much care for green veggies like broccoli. But broccoli in the shape of himself plus a zesty, cheesy sauce definitely changed his mind. And now he's the most important Gungan of all!

INGREDIENTS

1	head fresh broccoli
1/4	cup shredded parmesan
1	cup cubed American cheese
1/2	cup milk
1/2	cup smoky barbecue sauce in a squeeze bottle

1. Using a vegetable steamer insert, steam the whole broccoli head in a stockpot until tender, 6 to 8 minutes.
2. To make Boss Nass's crown, sprinkle the parmesan into an 8-inch nonstick sauté pan. Form the parmesan into a triangle in the pan, making sure the cheese is spread evenly. Place the pan over medium heat and allow the parmesan to cook and melt. When the cheese is bubbly and starts to brown on the underside, remove pan from heat. Slide the parmesan crisp onto a work surface. Carefully mold the triangle into a cone shape by rolling one side of the triangle to meet another side. Don't burn yourself! Press the seam with your fingers and hold in place until the parmesan crisp hardens and holds its shape.
3. In a saucepan or a bowl in the microwave, heat and stir the cubed American cheese and milk together until the cheese is melted and the sauce is smooth.
4. Place the steamed broccoli on a plate. Spoon the cheese sauce around the broccoli and place the parmesan crown on top of it. Squeeze swirls of the barbecue sauce onto the cheese sauce to look like Boss Nass' coat and draw the indentations in his crown.
Serves 2

Bubble City Salad

This shimmering salad evokes Otoh Gunga, the magnificent underwater city. Use a knife to serve up some Gungan-size slices of this cool, refreshing salad.

INGREDIENTS

1	large package lemon or pineapple Jell-O
3	cups water
2	packages unflavored powdered gelatin
1	can lemon-lime soda
12	large green grapes, washed
	Orange slices (optional)

1. In a mixing bowl, mix together the Jell-O and gelatin. Bring 2 cups of the water to a boil. Pour the boiling water over the Jell-O mixture and stir until dissolved. Add the remaining cup of cold water and the can of soda and stir.

2. Pour the Jell-O into the tallest, narrowest bowl you have and place it in the refrigerator.

3. After the Jell-O has set for about $1\frac{1}{2}$ hours, remove from the refrigerator. Using the handle of a wooden spoon, press the grapes into the Jell-O, suspending them at even intervals.

4. Put the Jell-O back into the refrigerator and allow to set completely.

5. When ready to unmold, dip the tall, narrow bowl into a sink or larger bowl full of hot water for 10 seconds. The Jell-O should release itself from the mold. Place a plate on top of the Jell-O mold and carefully flip it over.

6. Serve Bubble City with orange slices, if desired.

Serves 4 to 6

Main Courses

Padmé Pad Thai

Here is a quick and easy dish disguised as a gourmet meal. You won't believe how easy it is to whip up a plateful of these flavorful noodles... and neither will your trusted decoy.

INGREDIENTS

¼	pound dried rice noodles (banh pho)
4	tablespoons vegetable oil
2	cloves garlic, chopped
¼	cup water
2	tablespoons fish sauce
1	tablespoon brown sugar
1	teaspoon paprika
¼	teaspoon cayenne pepper (optional)
10 to 15	shrimp, cooked, peeled and deveined
4 to 6	scallions cut in inch-long pieces
4	tablespoons roasted peanuts, coarsely chopped
2	cups bean sprouts
1	lime cut into wedges

1. Soak the noodles for two hours in cold water or ½ hour in hot water. Drain.
2. Measure and chop all the ingredients and set them near the stove.
3. Heat the oil in a wok or large nonstick skillet over medium heat.
4. Add the garlic and stir for a minute.
5. Add the noodles. Cook them for about three minutes, stirring constantly and pulling them apart.
6. Add the water, fish sauce, sugar, paprika, and cayenne pepper, stirring to coat all the noodles.
7. Add the shrimp, scallions, peanuts, and bean sprouts.
8. Keep stirring and cook for about three more minutes.
9. Serve with lime wedges on the side for squeezing over the top.
Serves 2 to 4

Nabooli Forest

Here's the Naboo version of a tabouli-style salad. Fill the celery "trees" with your favorite spread and perch them in the landscape. And make that forest thick—you'll need all the protection you can get when the Trade Federation starts their invasion.

FOREST FLOOR

1	teaspoon olive oil
¼	cup diced yellow onion
½	teaspoon garlic powder
½	teaspoon salt
1	teaspoon lemon juice
1¼	cups water
1	cup instant couscous
2	tablespoons chopped fresh parsley
1	tablespoon chopped fresh mint

CELERY TREES

8	celery stalks with leaves
½	cup hummus, cream cheese, or peanut butter

1. In a saucepan, heat the olive oil over medium heat. Add the onions and sauté for 5 minutes.

2. Add the garlic powder, salt, lemon juice, and water, and bring to a boil.

3. When liquid is boiling, add the couscous. Cover and remove from heat.

4. Allow to stand for 10 minutes, remove cover, add the parsley and mint, and fluff with a fork.

5. Meanwhile, cut four of the celery stalks to the same length. Cut the other four stalks to the same length also, but longer than the first four.

6. Fill four of the stalks with your favorite filling.

7. Match each stalk with its mate and squeeze together.

8. Stand the celery trees up in mounds of Nabooli and enjoy!

Opee Sea Crunch

This delectable fish filet has a galactic crunch you won't be able to resist. Just watch out behind you — there's always a bigger fish!

INGREDIENTS

1	cup corn flakes
$\frac{1}{2}$	cup crispy rice cereal
2	tablespoons flour
1	teaspoon salt
1	egg
2	teaspoons water
1	pound fresh or frozen boneless catfish, sole, or bass filets
	Tartar sauce

1. Preheat oven to 350°F.
2. In a bowl, mix the cereals together and crush with your fingers into a coarse meal.
3. In a second bowl, mix the flour and salt together with a fork.
4. In a third bowl, whisk the egg and water together until smooth.
5. Take a fish filet and dredge it through the flour, coating evenly. Then place the floured fish in the egg wash and quickly coat both sides. Next, lay the coated fish filet in the cereal mixture. Carefully lay the fish on a baking sheet lined with parchment or foil. Repeat with the remaining fish filets.
6. Bake for 20 minutes. Fish should be cooked through and the breading lightly browned.
7. Remove from oven and serve with tartar sauce.
Serves 4

Sando Aqua Monster Soup

Deep in the recesses of your soup bowl, hiding behind chunks of celery and carrot, lies the sando aqua monster. Slurp with caution!

INGREDIENTS

1	large can (49 ounces) chicken stock
1	large jicama, peeled
1	cup chopped celery
2	large carrots, peeled and sliced into rounds
	salt and pepper to taste
1	teaspoon fresh thyme leaves (or $1/2$ teaspoon dried)
1	large can (10 ounces) chicken meat, drained (or 1 cup cooked chicken meat, chopped)

1. In a large stockpot, bring the chicken stock to a boil.
2. Cut the peeled jicama in half. Set one half aside and dice the other into $1/2$ inch squares. You should have about 1 cup diced jicama.
3. When the stock is boiling, place the chopped vegetables in the pot and boil for 10 minutes.
4. Remove from heat and add the salt, pepper, thyme, and chicken.
5. Cover the pot.
6. Have an adult carve the sando aqua monster out of the other half of the peeled jicama. Lay the jicama on the flat side. Cut four legs out of the bottom, then trim the rest of the jicama away to leave a long, slender body with four legs and a long tail (see photo).
7. Place the sando aqua monster into a large glass bowl. Carefully ladle the hot soup into the bowl and place it in the middle of the dining table.
8. Serve the soup with a ladle, but be careful not to be caught by the sando aqua monster!
Serves 4

Darth Double Dogs

Once you get a grip on these, you'll never go back to the single dog again.

INGREDIENTS

8   foot-long hot dogs

1   package refrigerator crescent dinner rolls

4   long wooden skewers

1. Preheat oven to 375°F.

2. Take a wooden skewer and skewer it halfway into one of the hot dogs, then take another hot dog and skewer it onto the other end. You will have one long hot dog held together with a skewer. Repeat with the remaining hot dogs.

3. Open the dinner roll package and unroll. The rolls will be perforated into triangular shapes. Detach them two at a time so you have four rectangles of dough.

4. Place one double hot dog on the edge of the rectangle, centering it. Roll the dough around the hot dog. When you get to the other side of the rectangle, gently press the hot dog down to seal the dough edge. Repeat with the three other double hot dogs.

5. Place hot dogs on a baking sheet and bake for 12 to 15 minutes, or until dough is golden brown. Remove from oven and allow to cool.

6. Serve with ketchup and mustard. Be careful when eating these — they are like a corn dog with a stick in the center.

Makes 4 double dogs

Pit Droid Pizza

Rumor has it that Watto's pit droids build these pizzas when they're not working on his Podracer. If they're in a hurry, they use prepared pizza sauce.

PIZZA SAUCE

1	tablespoon olive oil
1/4	cup chopped onions
1/2	teaspoon minced garlic
4	tomatoes, diced
2	tablespoons tomato paste
1/4	cup water
1/2	teaspoon each dried basil, oregano, and thyme, or double the amount of fresh, chopped
1	teaspoon salt
1/2	teaspoon pepper

PIZZA

1	cup fresh pizza sauce
1	pre-baked pizza crust
1/2	cup mushrooms, sliced
1/4	cup black olives, sliced
20	pepperoni slices
1	cup shredded mozzarella

1. Preheat oven to 375°F.

2. In a large saucepan, heat the olive oil over medium heat until hot. Add the onions and garlic and sauté for 6 minutes, or until the onions are soft. Add the tomatoes, tomato paste, and water, bring to a boil, then reduce heat to a simmer.

3. Cover the sauce and simmer for about 15 minutes, until thick.

4. Add the herbs, salt, and pepper, and stir. Remove from heat.

5. To assemble the pizza, spread 1 cup sauce on the center of the crust, leaving 1/2-inch or so around the edges.

6. Sprinkle half the mushrooms, olives, and pepperoni evenly on top of the sauce.

7. Sprinkle the mozzarella over the pizza.

8. Arrange the remaining toppings on top of the cheese. You may sprinkle additional herbs on top as well.

9. Bake on a pizza pan or cookie sheet for 15 to 20 minutes, or until cheese is melted and sauce is bubbly.

One pizza serves 3-4

Protocol Droid Pasta

Oh, my! C-3PO's parts are definitely showing in this delightful dish. Have fun decorating your pasta à la C-3PO, and don't forget the photoreceptors. A protocol droid needs to see!

INGREDIENTS

4	ounces dried multi-colored pasta (cappelini or spaghetti is best)	1	teaspoon salt
1	can (14 1/2 ounces) low-fat chicken stock	2	slices white or sourdough bread
2	cauliflower florets (fresh or frozen)		Olive oil
1	cup water		Garlic salt
	Pinch of turmeric	1	tablespoon parmesan
		2	pine nuts

1. Prepare the pasta according to package instructions.
2. While the pasta is cooking, pour the chicken stock into a sauté pan and bring to a simmer. Cook for 4 to 6 minutes, until the stock is reduced by half.
3. Place the cauliflower, water, and turmeric in a pan and boil for 5 minutes on the stove.
4. Turn on the oven broiler or toaster oven. With a knife or kitchen shears, trim one slice of bread into the shape of C-3PO's head plate and the other into a mouth plate. Brush both sides of each piece with olive oil, sprinkle with garlic salt, and toast in oven until browned.
5. When the pasta is cooked, drain and place it in a large bowl. Pour the reduced chicken stock over the pasta and sprinkle parmesan and salt on top. Using tongs, toss the pasta until coated. Mound the pasta onto a plate in a face shape.
6. When the cauliflower is cooked, place the florets slightly above the center of the face for eyes. Place a pine nut in the center of each floret to make pupils.
7. Place the garlic toast head and mouth plates as shown.
8. Sprinkle with additional parmesan and enjoy!
Serves 2

Desserts and Treats

Hideous Sidious Sorbet

Here's the scoop: icy and cold as the Sith Lord himself, this sorbet is surprisingly sweet. But like Sidious, it has the power to melt away without a trace.

INGREDIENTS

½	cup sugar
3	cups frozen blackberries, drained
½	cup berry Italian soda syrup (any kind of berry will work)
2	tablespoons lemon juice
½	cup heavy cream
1	sheet grape or berry fruit leather

1. In a blender, purée the sugar and berries until smooth. Strain the purée to remove seeds. Rinse the blender, and pour the berry purée, syrup, lemon juice, and heavy cream into it. Blend until mixed.
2. Freeze in an ice-cream maker according to manufacturer's instructions.
3. To serve, place two scoops of the sorbet in a bowl. Cut the fruit leather into four equal pieces. Drape the fruit leather over the sorbet, 1 piece per bowl, to resemble Darth Sidious's hood.
Serves 4

Watto-melon Cubes

Jedi mind tricks won't work on that tough-talking Toydarian, but these luscious cubes of melon just might. Take a chance on these juicy treats and let fate decide.

INGREDIENTS

½   large seedless watermelon

    Blue decorating sugar

1. Cut the watermelon into 2-inch-wide round slices. Trim away the rind. Cut the melon into 2-inch-square cubes.
2. Gently dab each side of the cubes on a paper towel to dry them slightly.
3. Pour the blue decoration sugar onto a plate.
4. Dip two sides of each cube into the sugar and place on a small plate, four cubes per serving.
Serves about 4

Anakin's Apple Crisp

The prophecy refers to the one who will bring balance to the Force, and there's nothing like yummy home-cooked food to give a kid a chance. You'll find that Shmi's original recipe produces a delectable dessert.

TOPPING

20	pecan shortbread cookies
1/2	cup flour
1/2	teaspoon nutmeg
1 1/2	teaspoons cinnamon
1/2	cup cold butter, cut into small pieces

FILLING

4	large green apples
3	tablespoons flour
1/4	cup sugar
1	teaspoon cinnamon

1. To make the topping, place the cookies in a zip-lock bag and crush them with a rolling pin into coarse crumbs.
2. Place the crushed cookies, flour, spices, and butter in a large bowl. With a fork or your fingers, crumble the ingredients together until the mixture has the consistency of pea-size clumps. Set aside.
3. Preheat oven to 375°F. Butter an 8 1/2 x 11-inch glass baking dish.
4. Peel and core the apples. Cut them into 1/4-inch slices, then cut the slices into wedges.
5. In a large bowl, toss the chopped apples, flour, sugar, and cinnamon together. Place the mixture in a baking dish.
6. Top the mixture with the crumble topping, making sure to completely cover the apples.
7. Bake for 30 to 35 minutes, until the topping begins to brown and the apples are bubbling.
8. Serve warm with vanilla ice cream or whipped cream.
Serves 6 to 8

Qui-Gon Jinn-ger Snaps

According to Qui-Gon himself, these cookies are an energizing nibble — the perfect pick-me-up for those times when you aren't busy battling destroyer droids or outrunning assault ships.

INGREDIENTS

4	cups flour	2	sticks butter
1	tablespoon ginger	2/3	cup brown sugar
1	teaspoon cinnamon	2	large eggs
1	teaspoon nutmeg	2/3	cup molasses
1	teaspoon salt	1/4	cup apricot jam
1/2	teaspoon baking soda	2	tablespoons powdered sugar

1. In a large bowl, mix the flour, sugar, spices, salt, and baking soda together.

2. In a separate bowl, beat the butter and sugar with a mixer until light and fluffy. Add the eggs and beat until creamy. Add half the dry mixture to the butter mixture and beat until well blended. Pour in the molasses and beat until mixed. Scrape down the sides of the mixer bowl, add the remaining dry mixture, and mix until well combined.

3. Wrap the dough in plastic wrap and chill for at least 1 hour.

4. Preheat oven to 350°F. Line two cookie sheets with parchment paper.

5. On a floured surface, roll out the dough 1/4 inch thick with a rolling pin.

6. Cut the cookies into rounds with cookie cutters. To make the door that Qui-Gon cuts through with his lightsaber, use the largest round cutters, and with a knife, cut small crescent shapes out of the center of half the cookies.

7. Bake for 12 to 15 minutes for softer cookies, 20 minutes for crispy ones. Remove from oven to cool.

8. While the cookies are baking, whisk the apricot jam and powdered sugar together until smooth.

9. After the cookies have cooled, spread 1/2 to 1 teaspoon of the filling on half of the cookies, placing another cookie on top to make a sandwich. Place the cookie with the crescent on top.

Makes approximately 20 small cookie sandwiches

Panakacakes

It's a good thing the palace tower wasn't actually made of these delicious, peanut-buttery cakes. Amidala and Panaka may not have been able to resist a nibble, and would have been delayed in their efforts to capture the viceroy.

INGREDIENTS

2	cups flour	1/2	cup milk
1/4	cup brown sugar	1	egg
2 1/2	teaspoons baking powder		Whipped cream or vanilla ice cream
1/4	teaspoon salt		Your favorite chocolate sauce
1	stick cold butter, cut into small pieces		
1/4	cup creamy peanut butter		

1. Preheat oven to 400°F. Line a baking sheet with parchment paper.

2. In a large bowl, sift the dry ingredients together.

3. With a fork or your fingers, crumble the butter and dry ingredients together until a coarse meal forms. (Pieces of butter are okay.)

4. In a small bowl, whisk the peanut butter, milk, and egg together until smooth. Pour into the dry ingredients and mix with a fork just until dry ingredients are moistened. Do not overmix.

5. Pour the dough onto a floured work surface and press dough into a rectangle, ¾ inch thick. With a knife, cut the rectangle into eight small rectangles. Transfer the small rectangles to the baking sheet with a spatula.

6. Bake for 20 minutes, or until light brown.

7. Serve with whipped cream or vanilla ice cream and chocolate sauce. You can also stack the shortcakes one on top of the other, layering the chocolate sauce and whipped cream between them. Then, with a serrated knife, cut slices from the Panakacake "wall" and serve.

Serves 6

Drinks

Sith Slush

This tart red spritzer with blueberry ice cubes echoes the sinister colors of Darth Maul himself. Picture Sidious and Maul cooling off after a long, hot day on the dark side with tall, frosty glasses of sparkling Sith Slush—cheers!

INGREDIENTS

½	cup blueberries or blackberries
1	can lemon-lime soda
¼	cup cranberry juice or fruit punch

1. In a blender, blend the berries until smooth. If not completely blended, add ¼ cup water. Pour the blended fruit into ice-cube trays and freeze.

2. When the fruit cubes are ready, mix the soda and juice together in two large glasses. Place two or three frozen fruit cubes into each glass and serve.

Serves 2

Bibble Bubble

Poor Sio Bibble had a tough job holding his own against Nute Gunray and Daultay Dofine. Rumor has it he calmed the nervous Niemoidians with a constant supply of this effervescent concoction.

INGREDIENTS

2	sugar cubes
1	tablespoon grape juice or Italian soda syrup
2	cans plain soda water

1. Place the sugar cubes on a soup spoon.
2. Carefully pour the grape juice or syrup all over the sugar cubes until they are soaked but still hold their cube shape.
3. Pour the soda water into two glasses.
4. Drop a soaked sugar cube into each glass.
5. After the sugar dissolves, drink with a straw.
Serves 2

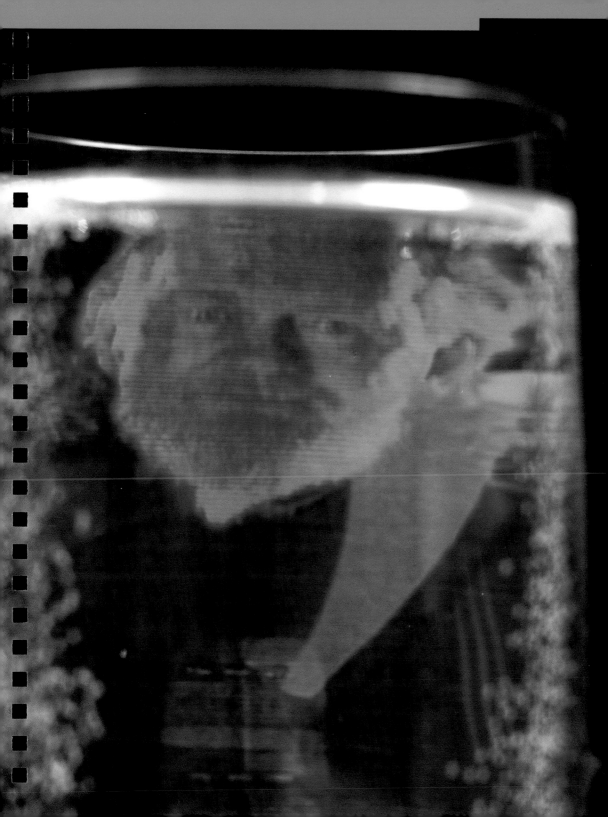

Sebulba's Sinister Cider

A cup of this steamy spiced cider will keep you
hot under the collar, just like the dangerous Dug.
It's a cozy warm-up on a cold winter's night.

INGREDIENTS

4	cups apple juice
$1/2$	teaspoon nutmeg
5	cinnamon sticks
4	whole cloves
	Whipped cream

1. In a large saucepan, combine the apple juice,
nutmeg, one of the cinnamon sticks, and the cloves.
Gently heat the cider for 10 minutes without boiling.
2. Place one cinnamon stick in
a mug. Ladle cider into the mug,
leaving the cloves in the saucepan.
Repeat with three more mugs,
and top each with whipped cream.
3. After the cider has cooled a bit, drink
through the cinnamon-stick "straw."
Makes 4 servings

Midi-chlorian Concoction

For a midi-chlorian count that's off the charts, we recommend a healthy helping of this tasty shake.

INGREDIENTS

1	banana
¼	cup creamy peanut butter
1	teaspoon cocoa powder
2	teaspoons sugar
1½ cups milk	

1. Slice the banana into a blender.
2. Add the remaining ingredients and blend 1 minute, or until smooth.
3. Serve in two chilled glasses.
Serves 2

Darth Malt

This milkshake is sinfully good, and the subtle malty flavor holds a certain mystery. Just a few velvety sips will prove how simple it would be to take the quick and easy path to the dark side.

INGREDIENTS

6	malted milk balls
2	large scoops vanilla ice cream (or your favorite flavor)
¾	cup milk

1. Place the malted milk balls in a heavy plastic bag. With a rolling pin or mallet, crush the milk balls into small pieces.
2. Pour all ingredients into a blender and mix on low speed until smooth and creamy.
3. Pour into your favorite glass and enjoy.
Serves 1

Index

Use this template ⟶
for Darth Maul Dip on page 20.
(You could also use it to decorate
a cake with Darth Maul's face.)

*To clean the template, wipe it gently
with a damp cloth.*